Other Books by Kerry Cox:

Collide-a-Scope
Rainbow Karma
Month of Sundays

Imagined Histories

Poems by Kerry Cox

To contact the author
or to order additional copies, please visit
www.kerrycoxpoetry.com

ISBN: 978-0-557-20963-7

For the late night dreamers wide awake...

a thick line

between loyalty and obligation
and it's
a thick line between forgiveness and fate
it's a thick line between my palms and my arms
where the scar tissue waits
it's a thick line between chivalry and misery
between girls who cringe when you kiss them
and boys who never cry
between violence and circumstance
between an orphan and an alibi
the line grows thin as crescent moon
between sympathy and sanctuary
the camel's back so close to breaking
and the bundles of butchered blessings you carry
the line thickens like braided rope
spun into compass cages
waiting for the unknown soldier
to be pressed into a name between pages
it's a thick line of seconds
between the lightning and the thunder
the sprinkled salvation on an infant forehead
and the wave that pulls you under
it's a thick line on maps
unnatural boundaries that hearts dare cross
between the fear of losing
and the actual loss
between hope and heaven
a trio of sixes or the fortune of seven
between the right and the wrong side of the tracks
it's a thick line between anticipation
and a surprise attack

the criss-cross cracks

a wire hanger can make in a child's back

it's a thick line between black plastic trash bags

and white satin purses

the coins that clang against each other

and the paper presidents whispering curses

it's a thick line of god's pencil

etch-a-sketching his will while we wait

tightrope tripping along the wire

and it's a thick, blurry line

between

love

and hate.

there goes god marching around my bedroom again...

there goes god
marching around my bedroom again
pumping that flag in his hands
up and down

a band of angels drum for god
in their flashy uniforms
outside my bedroom window
snare bass cymbal crash
and i swear i hear trumpets
coming from the closet

i turn over
cover my head with my dusty pillow
drowning out the epiphanies
the pile-driving of god's ageless knees

i bite the inside of my bottom lip
until i taste the g u i l t s a l t r e d
(knowing he's parading
right through my dirty clothes
crumpled papers
empty cups)
i pray for sleep
wondering if he can hear me
through all the ruckus

it's way past midnight
but god is immune to daylight saving time
or alarm clocks

sometimes i stare in disbelief
sometimes i escape firestyle
into a nightmare
ironically
there's some comfort in fear,
in the familiar

then god turns on the radio
starts scanning the dial
for something suitable
settles on the blues
he closes his firefly eyes
and sways back and forth like tall grass in rapture
but his feet still gently march in place

i'm glad it's saturday night
and i don't have to get up
early in the morning
(not that i sleep all that much
even when he's not playing cavalry
across my old blue carpet)

tonight i lay here
under a blanket of heavy heat
and wonder
if he could fix the air conditioner
but decide that's probably not something
you can ask god to do
besides
he seems awfully preoccupied
with the marching thing
and i wouldn't want to
interrupt.

a hatchet in her hands

joyce woods.
i can't forget that name, joyce woods.
she kept telling me her name and the date it happened.
she was walking in the highway at night when i saw her
and stopped, picked her up sometime after one a.m.
offered a ride to joyce woods
walking down the centerline of an underpass
with her expensive church dresses and shoes
in a plastic bag, and we drove
me and joyce woods and she was shaking, barely dressed
bare brown shoulders and shifting eyes
my car is on empty and she needs something
her daughter threw her out of the car on drugs, joyce says
'just went crazy and left me there with nothing but this bag of clothes'
and i fill up the car with gas and joyce is inside the gas station but she won't come out
and i'm so tired 'please joyce woods, i'll drive you home but we have to go now'
and i gave her some crumpled dollar bills
and her old hands pulled more from the plastic bag
her daddy died, she told me, her eyes glistened tears
and she bought some bottle of cheap liquor for his grave
'tomorrow is father's day,' joyce says, 'and i'm going to see my daddy'
and she says he was murdered and she tells me things i don't want to know
i'm leaving out the part she won't stop saying, 'i was raped,' she says, 'one month ago
he came in my house and he put a knife in my belly
and if i see that motherfucker again (i have a hatchet)
i'll cut him up that sonofabitch! oh i'm sorry ma'am!'
'it's okay,' i say and she's hungry but decides to wait until morning
and i drive into a deserted neighborhood
'my name is joyce woods, (turn left here) it was the middle of the night
and he broke through the door
and he was in my room and he raped me, young guy, about 24,

and i could tell he lifts up weights,

strong arms and he says *i been watching you joyce woods'*

and we pull up next to a small white shotgun house

and there's no electricity 'but i have a hatchet,' she says

'i'm just gonna sit here on the porch til it gets light out'

and i help her with her bag and she smiles

she has deep, dark eyes

she is wise and weak and she needs something

she is hungry so we go back to the drive-thru

and joyce woods spends her last dollar on a spicy chicken sandwich

and we are on the porch again and she eats like an animal

mouth full and talking and she moves her hand towards the basketball court

'he musta been one of those guys that hangs out there

cuz he said he's been watching me'

and the house was being swallowed by the ground and i couldn't leave her like that

'you have your hatchet, joyce?'

'oh! it's inside do, you think i should get it?'

'well, yes,' i say and there's a padlock on her door and inside is incredibly dark

and i am full of fear - i can make out giant holes in the floor, loose boards

sink pulled out from the wall in the middle of what might pass for joyce woods' kitchen

and inside feels like a trap, i switch on my tiny keychain flashlight barely breathing

she squeezes her thick body between a gap and there is her bedroom and it is a trap

there's only one way in and we are inside, we are trapped if anyone comes

i am trembling, her bed is there in the corner

'this is where it happened,' she says, 'he threw me down on that bed

and put my leg up on his shoulder

i told the police but they didn't find him yet

he came in right through this door - now i nailed it up'

'where's the hatchet,' i ask shining my feeble flashlight around in the filthy dark

and she suddenly remembers it's on top of the fridge and i reach

and there it is small and rusty

not the best weapon for an old black woman sitting on her porch

in the middle of the night

and she keeps talking

'i think we should get out of here,' i say and we do and she locks the padlock

joyce woods sits down in her chair with her hatchet there beside her

a bag of expensive clothes and shoes

barely dressed, thick arms, humid new orleans summer clinging

and a bottle of liquor for her daddy

'tomorrow's father's day, my name is joyce woods and i'll be fine,' she says

and i know i can't leave her here like this, i know i should **do** something

but there's a babysitter and i'm late and the kids are all sleeping

and i have that big empty bed to go home to and i tell her i'll come back to check on her

and i get in my car and drive away and i can't look back, i never go back

but i can't forget her eyes

i can't forget joyce woods.

300 words for snow

the Inuit have 300 words for snow
and i trace them all in capsized
calligraphy along
your sleeping spine

small snowflakes of brush-stroke
anuviak
the word for the snow
that remains in depressions on a hill
after the other snow has melted

trickling tears of temperature
kussaks, or
icicles building fences
against a barely blue sky
i see it all through your eyes

breathing life into letters
piqsiq - a blizzard
of blasphemy, i have
the godkiss
still wet and melting
on these lips

trembling hands
spilling your skin with
the sounds of new snow,
sugary snow
and snow with a frozen surface
after the spring thaw

we speak what we know
the way we, if drowning in dryness
of a desert life,
might have 300 words for sand

in a language of loss
i listen when you breathe out
and become accustomed
to the rise and fall
the familiar ways your heart has
of describing rainsounds
drizzle, shower, downpour
storm

and the ghosts of girls that
come to haunt you when
sleep is staring back
from the rearview
with wide white eyes

the refuge, the water
falling frozen

are erased
one still smudge at a time
down tired trails
revisited by pen
as i move left to right
reading in between the lines
of every word
i did or didn't

write.

eve's revenge

i like the way you
paint me out to dry
a sidewalk chalk monalisa

you're tall enough to be my mirror
old enough to be my 4 month younger twin

except your eyes
are not origami unfolding
they are something warm on the stove
but i like the brushes you use to color me in
or
sometimes a dull pencil you sharpen
to write stories about this salem snow white
burnt to ash on a wednesday
while mouths tasted
ebony becoming smoke

the priest who never kneels
spills
i heard that you camouflaged your confessions
when you begged him
with your biblical name
as a man of god
as a boy of questionable motives
to find out for you

if the 4th of july juliet
who made fireworks in your mouth
still somewhere breathed

still held the title
of fairest, most fucked up of all

but i came back to life for you
swam up from the bottom of the mississippi river
in the dead of night next to a ferry dock
pulled myself out
by a split black umbilical
payphone cord
like an off-broadway ophelia

smudged black and occasionally blue
and weren't you relieved that in our shakespearean tragedy
my resurrection kept you alive, too?

a clown-faced cleopatra
smiling at snakes that squeeze
me into every passerby's
imagined history
aging lolita with a candymouth
way of shaping words so that they
merge into things i do with my hands
when you're too afraid to look

it's too quiet
i need a horse
and an army of acrobats
to concoct a scheme
to get me out of here
a mint julep joan of arc
ready to lead my fog-fed forces
into battle with the blasphemy
of blood at the end of your bed

start with a fact

and build a misogynist mystery

"there's a wall in china..."

that i wear as a garter belt

full of tens and twenties

up on a table nearer my ceiling fan and god to thee

dancing in and out of wilting flowers

like the virginmary on ecstasy

you're wearing a bulletproof vest

you think i can't see

under all your brandname bravery

with your glass slipper soul

and hunter's box with a heartshaped hole

you pretend will fit anybody

but when i start the alphabet

i work my way back from Z

and right about now i'm flying from D to C to B

right up to the scarlet A that gets in the way

of your soon to be injured achilles

i like the way you marilynmonroe me

over your heater vent

and when i'm falling from the tops of tall buildings

you everytime capture me loislane-style

in mid-air uncannily

never seeing the delilah scissors

i hide behind my back

waiting

waiting

for you to fall asleep.

unlearning autumn's litany

i ghostwrite
abacus figures
in dust
in ash

on bars of soap
blemished with
dead characters
from egyptian aches

i feel this foreign fight
in the marrow of margins

i live in split-level
steamengine
stovepipe
solitude

grab me
i won't scream, i've practiced how

more lethal than your
sweet smell, boyish and baffling
i was left to wander in your
crevices
burn up as fever
your upper lip
beaded with my

wet-heart-heat
throbbing like minutes

this magnitude is a magic
mathematic
quiver

reverberating through membranes
people forget they have
until the hum keeps them (like me..
awake-at-night

guarded, graying
in these hush/hours
lidded and long

the longest scroll
of sadness a man
could write without
perishing in a winterdeath

icewhite
hands.hold.hemlock
a poison is a treasure
to the tongue of a lover

that has no one
left

to love.

the meek shall

goliath made me get on my knees
he had no teeth and i had no
excuse or disease
fortunate and bold
i learn the lies the latin told

another roman emperor trying to get away
these twists are the kind of mysteries
that could ruin your day

black shadow cliche
my left heel is torn open
and i'm too tired to run away

glib and dastardly
your smile haunts the crevices
between my rocks and hard places
i buy stamps just to look at the unblinking faces

garbage like a dump, a truck,
a rut the soul gets stuck in
i bought some of those pretty silky stockings
that i could get lucky in

so i may be angry and amberstuttering in my sleep
but no one can understand the words
or pay for the pension on the secrets they keep

i gave up glass slippers for soft-soled shoes
my throat grew tight in some sulphuric scenery
so that i could only whisper my moccasin blues

your mama had mine over for dinner and what do you know? she never came home.
i wasn't surprised, she hated the sight of herself sleeping alone

and i fell in love with a man who looked like a christmas tree
smelled like pinecones, broken bones and chamomile tea

married on the fourth of september below the asphalt sting
of a whiteness too cold to remember

now the weak have turned monthly, my mistakes crowd the crows
that i keep on the shelves in my room, in uneven rows

little stones, little slings
the giants fall
from the smallest

things.

you don't come around

skin shed the blood red
you don't come around

we were angry all night long
you slept 5 feet away
in bed

found a new way to pretend to be dead and

i memorized all the things you
never said

don't tell me lies
about where you've been
about how your eyes got red

you don't come around
the fire went out and i woke up cold and
my skin was blue
like my skin
was dead

i hid my secrets
my mouth from you
and my shoes
under the bed

don't say you're sorry
because i get lost in your voice
and forget whatever it was you
said

i told you i never can sleep on my back
and i can't escape from the wallpaper
you put up
the blackness inside my head

you don't come around

and i ride the carousel with all my courage
i feed the pigeons old stale bread
like an old lady with a black scarf
hiding the holes in my head

on fridays
or days when you haunt me
the scarf is white

and when i want to bleed
but can't touch a knife
i dig out the one in the bottom of the drawer
where i used to keep your picture
and it's a deep scarlet red

i go to the spot where we were going to meet
and i sleep there waiting for you
to unbreak every promise you said

i whisper prayers to a savior who's been hung and hushed in a hole and ascended
like things will do once they are dead

i dream of snake bites and fistfights and peace pipes
i dream i'm underfed
bulging belly of malnutrition
shaking in a makeshift basement hospital bed

porcelain hands hold cotton cloths to my
feverish head

the scars signal the stops, the lines, the lessons
outlined in red

like a map of rivers, like the channels on mars
made of tears of unknown eyes gone dry
like the ones you refused to shed

and i have no blame or game or shame
or guilty conscience or

faults and accusations left unsaid
in an architecture of understanding

i let you off the hook one last time

and just like a felon...

you fled.

this 4 letter morning

my feet cramped in shoes
yesterday i was living the after-effects
of a bad dream
on a bus
where the driver
wouldn't let me
get off

the day is still quiet
a few cars whirring by
on the distant road
that strange early light
slanting into my bedroom
where i wait in white down
to get up

in the river, i held
a heavy stone
walked along the sand
on the bottom
eyes open to see
what was there and wasn't
getting closer
looked up to mountains, sky
trees, blinking silver leaves
flecks of old gold below my feet
feeding on fruit
famished familiar
feelings
watching strangers
laugh and get wet

in this dim silence,

i remember all the moments

that gave me the courage

to sit up straight

on a sunday

without wavering

or a need

to get even

tonight if i dream

it will be of pomegranates,

secret staircases,

a wide river

and a way

to get across.

laundry list

manic it's understood
girls are crazy
hysterical

mooncheese champions
chilled with champagne

addicted to pretty glass
porcupines
things that pierce
pineapples

angry like tulips bobbing
their streakface heads in bantered
breathing

smooth it's understood
girls are spoiled
children who don't want

to grow up, to burn holes
in their pants with
broken lighters
arch upwards into chalkdust
blue sky trampled purple
like bruises on backs
that once were white
like china

that never got used
unbuttoned

it's understood
that girls scream
for no reason
unlace lockets from their
silhouette necks
pastel mints on grandmas' tables
good enough
to eat

angelfoodcake clamped
in mouths of matriarchs
mistletoe mistakes marrying
monsters
of some kind

ill-will and starspangled stains on
the carpet
that won't come out
the cost of keeping
half
of everything
including
a heavenbent
readytorent

heart

beating
it's understood
girls are

...

church closets

in all the corners
god paints himself into
the weary cross dressers
come bearing gifts of almonaster
and angry oils
befitting a child

a king to be born
and the mangers sit in silence
feeding the dark

in all the lofts
the soft clucking
of hay and animal dreams
float down softly
from jacob's ladder
to the final resting place in
the womb of a blessed child
with absentblue eyes
begging to be euthanized
by a spirit of holy handshakes
kisses on the lips
one man to another
a vase cracked to heal
the water it cannot hold
the empire falls
one drop at a time
into the riverbed gone dry
from so many partings
in all the marshes where
wildbirds blush

with the tinge of shellfish

and catechize streaks of gold

into a sky left on its own

to chameleon corset the world

in risky rays of splashing spectrums

low peach pie parading

across the tips of mountains

like stepping stones

anticipating tiny tangerine toes

the caves are batwashed black

hovering in hangars

where planes are erased in bermuda circles

and no one finds the wreckage

the fairytale fuselage or cathedral trains of wedded white

sweeping the petals from flowergirl fingers

along an aisle of regrettable red

and the confessional borrows the bars

of the bordellos

the windows and wielding of

salvation parsed out

one minor miracle at a time

at a tempo slower than god

with his brush

on the floor

painting himself

into corners

where cobwebs

used to think

they owned

the world.

ursa minor

for renee youngbear

ambershot delila
come down with me
to the fields of endless grasshopping

too much time on our hands
to much writing on our hands
too much blood
on our hands

talk to me
brushedup ballerina
of the moment
when your eyes
were more than eyes
but less than cracked open heaven

i will still listen
if you stop screaming
i will bury myself in the
space in between seconds
if the taste
rolls along my tongue
like the black between stars
don't swallow me tonight
cleopatra of crushed velvet
packed between layers of glass about to shatter

we watched our mothers burn
we felt them explode
we faded until we mimicked the ashes

and skin was smoke
curling like clouds just forming

your blood is not my blood
i hear drums when i sleep
but your father did not dance into death wearing feathers
even if i wished it so

my pineneedle princess
i carve you a cradle
for your sadness and rock
i am this ocean of a girl
breaking into invisible waves
no one knows where it begins
no one knows what we have lost

shine in this damp envelope
let the violence find its own beauty
in a brilliant flash of fury
calibrated tornado souls
spin side by side

lay beside me
like a lemon-scented lolita

i collect your soul in my hands

a stone,
a feather,
and your grandmother's ring.

still standing

that's how it happens when
you aren't really finished
and you're trying to save little pieces
of other people's heaven

you're trying not to listen
to the nightly news
or the buy one get one free sale
licking cake from your fingers

full and famished at the same time
the green gone dull in girlglint eyes

hips holding hula hymns
just under the cloth
of a birthday skirt

and we're blowing out candles
letting these minutes
tell the times of our lives

we're our own generation
of wreckless dreams
splintered wood
swimming lessons
we have these lifelines
dangling from our necks
like summer towels
albatrosses
empty lockets

we are

i am a collection of empty journals
a wishbone broken perfectly in half
an unfinished sentence

i used up all my words on a litany of nonsense
and was left standing
with unsalvageable sins
stillwater eyes
and enough garagesale guilt

to keep me from
confessing
to a god who
can't climb down
into the floods
falling from
his fingers

equilibrium

are those your handprints on the wall?
the child, the child
who likes to fall

the bruises apple-size and then
bruises underline your ribs again

someone turn me over
so i can see the light
someone give the cat some milk
and teach me to be afraid of heights

slivers in the palms
like a little saint with sails of gold
building paper ships to float
away from hands that halve the wholes

aristocratic smiles we share
among these china cups and plates
among the tarnished silverware
the whores who swallow syrupy love
the virgins who feast on empty hate
it's not the blackness brings you near
a warlord breaking blood in a glass
it's not who or what came first
history written by the illiterate last

in the guillotines of a hardened heart
the picnic tables, the worlds apart
sometimes my handprints stain the wall
a sunday's child after all

my mother drinks the devil down
her children iodine-stained at the knee
she paints the sting so beautifully

no wonder the child,
the child likes to fall.

simple degrees

He sat there talking about monarch butterflies. I was transfixed. The smell of oranges was everywhere. The air seemed still and yellow, almost butter, melting by simple degrees.

Everything was hum. I couldn't help but think of icicles melting drip by drip. Artificial rain. That's the way my mind works. Simple degrees.

We put up the tent together, or...I put up the tent and he watched from the picnic table, feeling slighted because my hands expertly slide the poles together as he fumbles apologetically.

The palm of my hand keeps getting caught in the plastic clips leaving a bloodpocket just under the skin. I show him and he looks away. Dark clouds combine with blue just overhead as the wind picks up, flapping the wings of the rust-colored tent. My eyes scan the temporary water of the nearby lake being whipped into little white peaks of meringue. Everything is backdrop.

The story is classical music. All violins and the smell of lightning drowning out oranges. That's the thing about electricity. Above the law of what should be. Sons of electricians won't go near the stuff. A legacy of fear forged through black burns in the fingertips. Horses in the barn stomp with restless legs.

Light shifts on water...and grass. We pull the tent tight, and into place. Three fabric rooms and a remote-control light. The rains come. The children shiver down into blue sleeping bags. His arms steel the pulse and something feels like a mouth at the back of my neck. Everything is forbidden.

The sky thickens, not that we can see it, but it's felt in the barometric pressure. The way veins slow to a trickle and the force of the night is pressing against rust and our own private air.

I'm lost somewhere else. The dry dust of Cherokee country is grain and grit when I blink and I stay closed as the waves pull up weeds in the lake 20 meters away, and it's all relative.

On another day, we'll watch clothes spin in dryers and the tent will stand empty and unafraid.

On another day, you'll threaten to leave and sleep slumped against the steering wheel. In a few months from now you'll mock a story you've always been told and use up borrowed favors to huff and puff against my windows as if anger alone could blow this house down.

No more rust, I've built a house of bricks. The tent lies sleeping in the trunk of my car. We were always an equation that didn't equal anything. You told me jokes and I was left smiling until your hands large and soft flicked against my skin in places not used to being touched and I was left with imperceptible bruises.

Now it's a Monday. We don't speak. Lions and lambs both lack courage and months are steamrolling their way toward something intangible. The smell of oranges. Everything blacktop. No one sees where the tent once stood or how you turned on your heel like thunder and screamed of my addiction to abuse, failing to see the irony that put you in the ring with me. You would return with an excuse. I would be ready. The tent was strong that day. New and arching with the power of my dollars. The ability to acquire the best. And a voice in my head that told me it was the right thing to do.

It happened in one fell swoop. And then again, it happened in simple degrees. He took you away from me. Or vice versa. Hindsight is so muddy. Eyes in the back of your head. You haunt nightmares like a devil who has nothing better to do. I still hear you laughing, or is that you screaming, everything, everything three times over. Like a curse, like a chant. Like a child who says I marry you I marry you I marry you. Expecting it to be so.

Possession is nine-tenths of the law. You dressed me head to foot in a black sari, thinking I was dangerous. Thinking I was attracting the attention of insects with my sweet skin and slow blood. You were right of course, I hung on the vine and ached for puncture. And release. The smell of ripeness, oranges, full of apologies, soaking your fingers. I would have escaped in a second, given a chance. Even now I'm pulling out pieces of my blanket from under your unaware body. Slow simple degrees.

Resigned to the fact, there are pieces I'll never retrieve. I watch the monarch butterflies pouring from his angel mouth. Shaped like a song. Morning caves into a sinkhole. I go, too. Obsessed with quicksand, stopwatches, leaves changing color, taxi cab meters, healing shades of skin, and silk cocoons unraveling a legacy more beautiful than what was borne from inside, like a seashell concocted carefully, one silent layer...

one mistake

one widening circle

at a time.

another romeo afraid of dying

[According to Reuters there was a newlywed couple in Iran who had sex before marriage. They felt so guilty about it that they entered into a suicide pact. The man "helped" his wife kill herself before chickening out on his end of the deal. He then turned himself in to the authorities.]

they say she lit her clothes on fire
threw herself down a well

they say she was afraid of tomorrow
and electricity

when they found her
your name was inked
all over her swanbody

the neck too curved
and paler than moonflesh

you have your alibi and white teeth
all smile and sorrow

looking through the bars of a
fairytale

what happened to the promise
the precision with which you climbed
to the balcony and brazenly broke
her heart open
so that you could taste
daybreak
through the mouth of a virgin

the trouble with ash is its ambiance
ability to shroud the sky

she lay like porcelain
in a glass drawer for days
and you didn't dare
to wake her with a biblical kiss
she went up like a burning bush

and who were you to question
her motives

bird feathers tainted with char and chisel
the sculpted sound of something torn

we watched the white gown of guilt turn tidal
at her ankles
unable to stop the unraveling of oxygen
and heat
consuming the costume
of her indivisible grace

i guess you hadn't heard the news
stomping around in your hero's shoes
glass slipper dreaming of a girl
who was easy to win
impossible to lose

but who ate brambles?
could a tourniquet turn off your
leaky heart?
the age of another ambivalent atlas

the globe spun slow blue-greens in her eyes
your addiction to filth and whiskey wishes
left you doubting

how you could touch the

tassles

of her erogenous smile

without becoming

stigma on her splash

of skin

so you walked

into the desert as if

the banished bite of losing everything

could restore her

and your eyes went clouds

camoflauging

the carnivore

how you were devouring

the last pieces

of a memory

the bliss of blue tinge

you tasted on shadowed lips

the girl gone statue

immortal

in the gauze of a long goodbye

and you stood there cowardly in the cup of her courage

the only one

who didn't need

to ask why.

villa nail

you drew a line in the sinking sand
i didn't dare to cross
i held a white flag in my hand

this isn't the way i had things planned
my fingers calculate the cost
you drew a line in the sinking sand

a love of sea and a love of land
a triple sided coin to toss
i held a white flag in my hand

now i can't say more than 'if' or 'and'
the rolling stones leave me their moss
you drew a line in the sinking sand

i wear the circle of your burning brand
the tide recedes to mourn my loss
i held a white flag in my hand

the distance that these hearts once spanned
the bridges burnt when we tried to cross
you drew a line in the sinking sand
i held a white flag in my hand

my gramma

Anna has faded away
into stars and brilliance
and i keep my middle name like a promise
to her

at 8 years old
i took forbidden photos
as she scowled
hating the camera
so that i had to trick her
with a mischevious grin
yelling out, "Gramma!"
until she looked my way
and the flash froze on her
surprised face
captured in my photo album

one day comparing
two photographs
from several years apart
she was wearing the same skyblue sweater
over her shoulders
top button buttoned
she was wearing the same apron
and white shirt under that

had become a caricature of herself
shouting angry words
scolding my father
or the dog
or both

her children now scattered to
seattle
florida
and places in between
never close enough

the blankets she crocheted with
an insane mixture of colors
out of yarn that took on
the property of lead
when woven tightly
into a thick
thick blanket

that's how she held us
from so far away
ginger ale in her fridge
the giant pot of spaghetti and meatballs
the cheesecake held like a treasure
on my lap
on the long plane ride home

the house with snow piled
all along the sidewalk
up to my little girl knees in the backyard

and her embarrassment
at the neighbors
calling her up
to report that a man
(my dad)
was cross-country skiing
down the middle of her street

mom said
she'll cry when she sees you
and she always did
I didn't understand then
why she would cry
if she was happy to see me
now, somehow
it makes perfect sense
the candles she always kept
from my dad's young venture
of his own candle shop
and the one i love most of all
water blue wax
coated in sand
with pools and wicks here and there
pieces of driftwood
tiny ceramic seagulls
where will it go?

the last time I saw her
she gave me old lady shirts
that i would never wear
but would never tell her
just thanked her
while looking at her shelves
her shrine of smiling pictures
the children,
all the children
smiling.

how she cried when she had to put the dog down for months after
how she hated the cold
and us on the other side of the country

us never coming to visit
the cards that came every christmas and birthday
without fail

the christmas cookies she sent
in boxes of bubble wrap
the crescent moons and chocolate chip
the oatmeal raisin and the surprise cookies
with the chocolate centers
cookies enough to last until easter
started to come later each year
our boxes the same as the ones she sent
to all her children
and children's children
and the story my mom told
of how when i was one
i choked on a surprise cookie
the surprise we didn't know about

so short she sat on a cushion
to see over the wheel
and the last time i was with her
she told stories
as we ate
of her young girl days
working in a diamond factory
and meeting my grandfather
that tall skinny irish boy
she almost passed up

and when she told me
how much
it hurt

her body hurt
and always the same words next
"but whaddya gonna do..."

rhetorical questions
that left me speechless
helpless
and still

always

even today

way too far away.

prayer for a mistaken savior

hang me on your cross
my hands need nails to keep them from shaking
a queen with a crown of my own making
the thorns in your eyes and
the tears i'm still faking

trap me in a hymn of angels
heal me with your floodstained hands
cut my heathen hair and hold me
leave me to drown in desert sands

i pushed these pillars
and i was blind
i burned all your bushes
to see what's inside

and it wasn't an eden
or an ark that could save me
goliath or lambs or a newborn baby
words written on stone
thrown down your mountains
a sea torn in half
coins baptized in fountains
it was a backwards warning of love
with a twist
water turned to wine
a caress with a fist
a betrayal
that shackles the heart and the wrist

in your borrowed pages
of thieves and the holy
you stab me with miracles
as if this would console me

and the wise men bring me gifts
of solitude and sympathy
suffocate my blasphemous mouth
just like you used to kiss me

you grew your heart into a stone
to cover my tomb and seal me away
3 days i'll lay and dream of you
then rise and walk away...

silencing science

albert einstein dreams of cubic zirconia
on his island of instruments

i raft about and relive my youth
while still managing to look
so young

pantomiming the birth of christ
i paint my eyelids blue for you

another maria, another damsel in distress
isaac newton masturbates upside down

vodka martinis with extra olives
dirty mouths and two ways to pay
cash or credit because
the big man says nothing is free
but i see the way he looks at me
me plus his anti-social wife makes three

every boy's favorite number

the filters are clogged with kleptomaniacs
returning merchandise for in-store credit
filing grievances to the security cameras

'i'm ready for my close up'

thomas edison used a flashlight
to find his way home after drinking
himself stupid on a saturday night

my skeleton is hanging neatly in the closet
behind my new winter jacket
the color of camels

come see how the carpet camouflages
the cashmere impersonation
of this miracle fabric circa 1972
even the tag brags of its
"luxurious surface"

alexander graham bell is accepting the
charges from miss cleo calling collect
to give him his free psychic reading

a cockroach the size of a shotgun shell
is now stuck to the bottom of my shoe
i'm stacking up the empty bottles that
built this tower of babel
and a headache the size of texas
if you cut off the top and bottom
and a little on both sides

bill gates is buying laptops
for the little girls in cambodia
so they won't have to walk the streets at night
he threw in the webcams no extra charge

i have one empty canvas and an old idea
of tracing around my hand with a pencil
or a permanent marker
eighty-seven times

i hung a curtain over the mirror

and left the window naked

knowing the neighbors like to see me practicing how to die

coloring my hair

reaching for the remote

to a tv i don't own

i can't figure out

why a boy never seems so heavy

lying on top of you kissing your freckles

as when you try to carry one

on your back down a city block

da vinci is spray painting the

side of a train

but no one can figure out

what it's supposed to be

and he says he hid the answer

in the mona lisa's mouth

you never know, he says

and i say sometimes you know

sometimes you drop your coffee cup
on the floor in the kitchen and it shatters
into ninety-six pieces
tangled in tea bags

sometimes the tears come
before the phone hits the receiver
and everything seems
whiter and brighter than it should be
all the goodbyes evaporate
clouds refuse to take shape
and it's monday
it's december
the speakers click and buzz
and you won't answer the phone

i'm just taking another bath in neon
my fingernails bitten too close
to the skin
and it's flashing through my windows
blue
pink
yellow

i'm eating streaks of doubt and indifference
it's the only thing that i have an appetite for

don't say destruction
i've been creating this pseudonym for years

so that when i told you how i felt
you couldn't pin me down

maybe my hands are a controversy
of right and left
and i am unborn
i am overdue
i am coming through the tunnel feet first

dirty hair and dandelions
another summer fetish
buttercup braids and these dresses
smelling like clothesline

alcohol, the sting and rub
the cottonballs
the needlestick
i'm inebriated with solitude
and plucking pirouettes from
my own ten-speed curls
lines that corrupt tornadoes
we are

the biggest afterthought

the month of may ever had.

body pictures

the shape of your thigh in my hand
makes an interesting conversation piece,
the composition
of your lips
against my palm
the texture
of heat blending into
tangled sheets
is pure genius,
the perspective from under,
the eyes smeared closed,
angle, curve
fingers tracing
back of neck,
the jealous film
grabbing the skin
pressing flesh flat
in a four-sided frame
no sign of movement

we still life
we breathe
hair drips onto
thirsty shoulders,
hips slide eloquently
through empty air,
turn, pose
shifting sounds left behind,
the cheekbone flush,
the captured canvas

painted perfectly,

we shrink and slip

inside the lens

a mirror, a microscope

an x-ray

to show how fast

your blood pumps,

the way the spine trembles

from a tornado of touch,

the depth of drunken desire

shadow and light

play across your face

the reoccurring dream

of your hands

pulling it all into place

before the rising

of a blind new day

brilliant sunspeak

pouring through clouds

through windows

leaving these pictures of our human puzzle

overexposed

forgotten souvenirs

of how a whisper

looks laying between

two photogenic hearts

as they echo

their conjoined sorrow

through cages of white.

older and wiser

(in memory of my heroes mother theresa and dr. martin luther king, jr.)

blame the basements in birmingham
holding the secrets of a revolution
blame yourself, young man
you just looked away again

cavemen cry over holes in the ozone
your mother cries over
things she can't control
everyone's crying into empty plates
hungry for things they can't
put on credit

tonight I put on my shoes and stapled the sidewalk into a
pamphlet complete with a political promise
to burn up all the funeral homes
and let the dead run free
don't blame me, young man
don't blame me

just keep coloring inside
the whitelines
of distraction
the money mistaken for passion
no one needs an education
under an asbestos roof
the lungs learn the lessons
of grandfathers deep in mines of
coughedup coal
that keeps you warm in winter
young man, that keeps you warm in winter

i'm not saying i don't believe your sincerity

your suit seems very credible

and the shoes alone prove your honesty

but trust is a commodity the 21st century can't afford

don't blame me

i'm not the architect

i just live in the building

and when I see the tanks roll by down my oaklined street

it makes me wonder at the size and shape of fear

at the color of forgiveness

and it makes me wonder where all the young men go

when it's time to pick up the pieces

of a coward's cavalry

don't shield your eyes

young man

it's not truth

if it doesn't hurt

come forth the angels

in everyday clothes

tear your skin into bandages

to heal the murderers

cleanse the whores

the mother of the dead and dying

singing lullabies and cradling

her poverty like a broken bird

smiling at the golden graves

remember the sounds of innocence, sacrifice

believe in a state of endless grace, young man

believe in what is hard to believe in

and march on, young man

with the brothers of dark beginnings

born from the earth's fertile dreams

unrelentless in a joyous scream

an arch of long fingers

a temple of captivity

blood on the floors

from the children who wake into nightmare zones

broken homes and stolen guns

hold them up high to heaven

young man, like the devilfearing doctor

in the bruised history of revival

walking like jesus

arms full of palm leaves and prayers

to teach those who lie still

to stand and walk again

have you seen the miracles

young man?

did you see the imprisoned prophet

die on a cross of concrete?

did you see the starving eyes

close one last time

or the warring souls

fall into a silent peace

did you have a hero

who could walk on water

or walk on air

young man

or

do you even care?

call yourself a slave

to commerce

and dead presidents will come to shackle you

call yourself stripped

of dignity

and watch your clothes disappear

call yourself lonely

and watch everyone walk away

but never call yourself

unforgiven, young man

when all you have to do is ask.

the pain lies

obscene

unseen

unclean

it's time

young man

it's time

to drop the mask.

if it weighs more than you think

i believe in the heaviness
of a person's soul
the dreams clumped up
at the back of the head

the shoulders slumped forward
the meat and muscle
grinding like gears

and i can be mesmerized easily
by the motion of fingers
quivering on keys of a piano
or scampering over strings
of an old guitar

like a cat i curl into my corner,
empty and alive
breathing hard like
wet horses in april

spotless, my conscience
when i think of what i need
the charms i used to nestle
at my neck
in my gratitude pose
looming like a lighthouse
a beacon
and a warning.

these shadows, curved
into an egg's oval outline

like a seed summering in soil
unable to bear fruit

clasped in hands, bells
that jingle golden
small words that get stuck
between teeth

i believe in gravity growing stronger
as we grow older
how these moments make up
unending symptoms of sicknesses
no one will name

blind apparitions
the faith and the acres
of these archaic measures
gospel songs slapped down
between the palms
dying trees
and the winter of a heart
grown white

these scales portrayed
by two small hands
opposite angles
and apples and oranges
comparing the measure
of feathers and iron
piling up like promises

while i am left weightless
yet heavy somehow...

another fool of april

and when
they called him a fool
he laughed with all his teeth
something more like
a limerick

bad breath and 3 days worth
of dented cars
tin can drums and falling
barometers

the noise seemed unbearable at moments
and the air felt like real fingers

and our mouths were cotton soft
ours heads laid on stone tablets

still unetched

and when he laughed
no one listened

the stagger and swagger of too
much time
on sidewalks
too many eyes turned away

we suffer through humidity
and hold up
hands full of humility

as his sins he advertises
on a handmade card board sign

we don't think about the black feet
of dirt dancing

the hair streaked with soaking salt and sun

of the fool laughing
with a bag full of bricks
to build a house

that no huffing and puffing
can quake
that all our empty prayers
won't keep
standing.

i miss something

that we never had,
matching watches, morning tea
on a wooden tray, strewn blossoms
messy hair, tv turned down low
we giggle at cartoons
we smudge the circle of heaven
between us, like black charcoal
like eye shadow and bruises
i give you
twelve of everything
march around the room
ready for invisible battles
clacking against your heart
my hand shivers
glows

in the green minutes
my hair gone straight i simmer your silence
your scent into soup
licking the spoon
that never solves the hunger problem
deep in the pit
of my plenty
courageous and drumming
pounding feet on sand, running
from the things we hate
smiling at jellyfish in the
silver skinned pacific
we share like a secret
i show you flashlight dreams on the
wall as you try to sleep

vanish in the 3 a.m. blush and fog
like lipstick faded from
fiery lips kissed into colorlessness

campfire stories, terrible colds
nestled in two tons of comfort
some september sunday
greedy for the fluid motion
of july burned into falling sparks
and juicy words that danced
on glass, bounced like hail
on the sidewalk

and swung like a lunchbox
at the end of my little girl

arm.

in other words

we danced in a widening circle
or-

i danced and you

shifted uncomfortably, arms and legs limp
in that emptied out
orb of concrete

surrounded by so many trees, raining
down around us
golden

leaves and memories, we climbed the fence
staring down into the cemetery
on the other side

reading names and dates of people long, long gone

in the conservatory with its giant windows you followed me
to the cactus room where the dry air
dizzied up the room
i took your picture here and there
looking for the carnivorous plants

listened to the children singing in a
circle in their yellow slickers

and lost my breath on the stairs
of the water tower.
come closer

now, i see some stars burning their way
through the october in the air
i open my mouth and taste the music
on my tongue.

rusted red the wheelbarrow's dead

so much depends upon a red wheelbarrow
full of rainsoaked chickens
gasping for whitewinged air
reminding us all that life is not fair

so much depends on your hands
tangled in my hair
the way your left foot hits the stair
the smell of you lingering in my room
even when you're not there

so much depends on
winter's wedding of white
with the red of a young girl's hair
the tiny temptations of snowflakes
on tongues that bleed in the air
cut into precision of a language
broken and bare
branches without leaves
without a trace of green
 to spare

so much depends on the wheel
invented to turn this world around
the indescribable gravity of hanging upside down
the black and white enigma of knees that hit the ground
and the sound...
the sound...
as you put
the telephone down

the echo gravel screech of tires
outside the window
the circular driveway
dreamed blacktop under fields so long ago
in a kansastype of dream
where we hide inside of cornrows
and the laughter
has nowhere else to go

the spiral of these unkempt curls
reminding you of a tornado
and the shelter
the shelter
down below

so much depends on things
we'll never know

recycledrainwater

sometimes it rains all day and the ground is still thirsty forgetting how to drink it all in sometimes the air is so thick breathing seems impossible and maybe for a moment unnecessary and when the falling sun prepares to surrender to the shaded blue of a quiet june night it sometimes seems to hover for a moment too long needing the attention and i can relate to that because sometimes i walk into a room and don't know why I'm there but i guess we all do that and sometimes when words wont come i wish i had another way to tell you how it is with me but a voice is not always just sound your voice is a thing alive that moves around inside me rolling me around like hightide waves or sometimes drifting across me like clouds lazy in their whiteness or maybe even fluttering inside me like a school of fish kicking up flashes of sudden silver and i am bound by the weather to remembering the silence of your stillness the thirsty sky the dry dirt under my feet the bible of your blue eyes and sometimes late at night i'm on my knees and you would swear i'm praying for rain

even Freud had nightmares

don't get out your
dream dictionary

i don't want to know why
i spent all night running from fires
i had made myself

dispel the myth
that i myself am angry
this is not red in rage
i pale to pink
and pretend to miss your nose

garbage trucks come early again
waking me from the one
where they held you hostage

and the knife i had made
would not pierce the skin
of anything

so i waited for real daylight
and crept back into
the dark room of sleep
to imagine my basket full
of cookies for your grandma
and my little red hood
kept sliding down my back
while the wolf behind the tree
sneered

there was a ripple of recognition
a recess from regret

i was gnawing on a telephone when it rang
and the only sound
was static

water streamed down the windows
sunday kissed me hello with
wine-soaked lips

put away your tarot cards
i'm the queen of my own cups

shattered like knuckles
that punch walls, fences
and sometimes
even
stone.

quote me

i'm saying nothing
again today

my lips move

my body moves
my feet moves
the earth moves
the air moves around me

and you stand

still

fire me
from this slavery
the shackles of silkscraped indifference
my fingers are bones wrapped in dry skin
worked down
worked through

and i keep ticking
inside
like a bomb
something keeps pumping through me
forcing me to go on
waves keep crashing
from inside my ribs
one two
one two

as you slip through pretending to move
as you mock me

buy all this beauty
pluck out the purchases
and lay them all down
they shine like stolen money
they shine like the inside of
something rotten

and you write me a letter
that looks like a map
to the mall of america
twelve miles long

my bed blames you for its emptiness
and the sun told me it burns me
because you asked it to
and your grandmother kissed me
as she was dying
something you would never do

i can listen
if thats a virtue
i can wait outside in the rain
i've been colder than this before
and i've obliterated the line between psycho and sane
i still choke on your name
and these pills all taste the same

quote me
i'm saying nothing again today

use it against me

i'm the only weapon you ever held

the only shot you ever fired

the only voice you couldn't hear

the only lesson you refused to learn

but i don't mind

cuz i houdini'd out of your handcuffs

and this time my getaway is clean

driving away so fast

you look like you're moving

backwards

goodbye, october

this jungle
garage
this faraway
mirage

tantrum told
bones cold
scars warm
eyes, a storm

gamble all this rushing
slush
on a tremble, a touch
landscape lush

like the dream
your drought-fed
mouth said

last time i told you
how hard it rained
when you left on the last
8:30 train

liar's choir

rehearsed your hollow hymns
until they started to sink in

another wild embankment
i can't climb

another set of whispers
that i just cant seem to rhyme

a dirty bathtub
full of week-old gin

blanket lies and wonder eyes
the milk of money sucked from the skies

here i am lost in a dream
of your...
purple thighs

don't ask me where i've been

your boldfaced artist-heart
drawn abstractly in its
expensive frame
on a white wall
collecting sideways glances
i can't swallow that temperature
lukewarm lunacy laced with
superstitious suits of afterhours style

you think i'm drowning
just because
i can't swim
but i risk the red entendres
and roll this into circle-seeking smoke
my thorns break at the touch
and i tell time
by the ticking silence
where the sound of clocks used to be

there's a hole in my night
that only you fit in

ignorant of fortune and its
bag of dirty tricks
and ambivalent to one-way streets
(and straight-up similes
with blacked-in eyes)
beauty walking down the plank
catsweeplong
and shotgunthick

i'd bet it all on amnesty
if i knew that i could win

velvet me in a loose-fit litany
like lost and tripped-up angels
looking for a faded cradle
bury me in a festival of feathers
i dream of waxen wings
as you collapse like curtains
all around me

inbreathe

the darkflush...

outbreathe

the barbwire fences

that unravel into passive

pieces of penance

now we can see the mistake-
white is the color of sin.

bare

i took you as is, cordially
hand in weathered hand

these gloves too tight
my mouth moving in slow motion

the branches stripped
all your words bricks through my windows

garbage truck mondays
these are the monsters of meaning i'm choking around
you have no sound when you stare
and space suspends the syrup
the sweet ways we learned to lick
on loose nights when the liquor ran clear
like water and honey

singing, your muscles struck a chord
and my afterthoughts gambled on red hearts
cut from paper, paper dolls black eyes
violence begets silence
when the solemn secrets of fingerprints
tell stories wherever they touch

pollution in me

a continent of walkaways
portraits painted
weatherized

we play these hurricane games
and strip the sheets that
stifle
the screams of bedpost
birthdays
and bundled bad dreams

something about the thiefstreets
the sirensick calls of men in blue
beating the black from artificial
turfs
angel rings when we slice these
trees to see how long
they waited to die

this is the hard level and the tools
are boxed and locked until some
harlem houdini tempts the teaspoons
and boils blessings into something
injectable
as if all we could fit in the
eye of a needle was
rich men and camels
waiting for winter
in a desert of disaster
and the oily smiles set forth
the fires

the barges undertowing
the illnesses of alleyways
comforting the cancer that eats
eats everything
until it's only bones
bones and borrowed black suits on a sunday
when priests are hard to come by

a continent of walkaways
learning to rewrite their names
as cuneiform
cinderstacked pyramids of coal
that will never develop anything diamond
never be baptized beautiful into
something worn on the fingers of
blushing brides
banished to burn in grates
and steam engines
as if time stood still
for ugliness
for ugliness and usefulness
that defies evolution
a revolution
of need

the holes in these sidewalks un
marked as if we hoped
the skinny souls would slip in
and disappear without a sound

cardboard resting places and
crutches for show

a black bicycle and buggies
and baskets blooming with
paperflowers, red berets
and iron oak timeless mocking
your thirty day sentence to
respite in spite of your
part time prayers
and candles named after
the suffering saints
on their knees just like you

a continent of walkaways
crossing over
blinking into bays and
shuddering at the thought
of sharkmouths
sharp shooters
the violence of asphalt and apathy
operatic operations left open
stitch stained skin where one half
never meets the other like it should
and the adjustment is accidental

something awake and official about your eyes
all the anger of an effigy
painted on in streaks
like a warrior toy in the hands
of a little boy that drums his doubts
into double fisted fury
as the time trails his ankles like tin cans
telling the world he's been
just married to the mistakes of a million men
he doesn't want to become

but these moments can peck away
at the power of an apology until
the neck is bruised with the things
we stacked in piles
the kind of kisses we burnt at the stake
at those points in history
where geography becomes a lesson
in lines on a map
stuck in a latitude longitude puzzle
that protects the guilty gravesites
your grandchildren
will be left to dig

sparks and scars

it's still there
creeping under the salted skin
more smoke and flame
your volcano voice

i still come
running at the sound
still swallow all your dreams
for the way they curl
inside me
comfortably

still shudder
shake, solve the
shameriddles
smile like a snake
still sigh like a song

swimming in circles
that aquarian sin
twin and twin
begging for breath
and water
you still tempt
tell secrets with silence
grab hold too tight
tease and try
those treacherous moves
still stomp across my
midnight
kicking up dust and doubt

jimmy the lock
to my bedroom door

still smell like the
dark room we met in
sparks and drums
between us

and the pounding
i still hear it
still feel it
separating us
and sometimes
holding us close

honey, it's not the weather

give up your guns
they jam and stick and
run
out of

ammunition

get wet and glisten
make it hard to listen

and don't walk so slow
making tracks
in the
snow

it's not that pretty of a show
when white
goes dirty

i'll play the game
blame shame pain
some parts of the south
are sunken under a
vast floodplain

and this is true
of the best minutes
i've spent
with and without

you

don't grovel
my gravel is imported from
rock quarries in maine

my best vein
slushes through me like your middle name

i have food in my hand
for the wild animal inside you
dreaming of a time
you'll sleep next to me
tired and tame

this is my indian summer
sung for sugar-fed bats
that clamor for a calmer
chamber

and i am andromeda
making love to the rocks and sea
spray

long ago having swallowed
the key
to unchain her

i can get by

in these blink

born, teeth-crushed
bluevelvet mornings
bells jar me awake

clouds cover my stomach
and wrench water from my
whitewrist

watch
climb the vine
columns combine
and i paint my muscles
like a lunatic
concubine

in these bored
bred
smoothfed
lines
snorted from mirrors by
candycane heroes
there is laughter
but no
true taste of what
shame sells

clipped wings
orange heart
terrible secrets and bad handwriting

a doctor dying
behind a door
and seven years more bad luck
a nip, a tuck
a fluctuation
in station

these radio waves
are washing up
on beaches while
the tone of the stones
own
outgrown home
is bruising
the breath

i am choosing
my most likely
form of death
like a coat
i can take off
and put on

craning this long neck
i swan
across the pond
dreams slivered until
gone

but beyond

before

because

beneath
i believed
grieved

i thieved orchestra
music
i threw it

the sound of the pages
fluttered for ages
i built a tempting cocoon
in silent stages

trembled in the afterbirth
of your wrangled rages

raw
these tales
take time to tell
and i can learn to
listen

to the stacks of starbirds
clucking in their cells
accustomed to the jampacked jails

cannonlaunched by pirates
pretending to sew more sails

while the dead men bang their bones
as loud as hell
when all else fails.

i was still listening

he's wearing a red hat
outside the hatstore
i have lipstick in my pocket
(not
onmylips-
core clap
stomp slap

vicious like a broom
sweeping up a room or
gloom

don't assume her
face
became a locket
by accident
--->
smoke-filled bite
a round a bout
outside the box
crossing
i found some tracks
that led to a shoulder
destined to smolder
like the ash mask of a central park boulder

you eat big
bleed small
dig spoon holes
through us all

grapple with trunktrees

drunkbees

busted like

kid knees

and my mama

made blue

seem sad with

iodine ink

i had a poem leaking from me

even before

i grew these

legions of loitering

licks on the page

with lips

that still don't

stick)-...

seller's remorse

the price was right
the jaw forgotten
dropping into an empty fishbowl
heading for the bottom
ten pence
less
than mixed flavored incense
tempting my room to tapdance

you were in a 3 piece suit and
i was one rose short of a dozen

could have been an accident
the way your hands jack-and-jilled against mine
may have been a circumstance of disaster
for me to come tumbling after

so let's sweep this under the rug tonight
in the empty bedroom
where the ropes are all tight
and deadends are dangling
everywhere in sight

i once burned myself free of the noose
of your nocturnal needs
well, tonight you look like you might

turn into a pumpkin when the clock strikes twelve
forgive me then
i'm not one to delve into deserts
looking for water

but this thirst is more like an addiction
to taste
and the rain is a ruckus
and i miss your face

i've got all this money
that you won't accept
i wake up to sirens
like a gypsythief suspect
and my fingers are inked
with the black of your ceiling
we share the same spectacles
with knees bound to bleed
from all of this kneeling

but i take turns
between begging and praying
kissing you goodbye
then dreaming you're staying

the hot commodity
imports and exports
you market your heart
and advertise the offer that i can't refuse
it's a 2 for 1 deal down on aisle 7
we'll throw in a free book
on how to get to heaven

well i still believe in most fairy tales
and my bedsheets are lined with softly crushed shells
and the thunder is supper and the rain is my vice
and i'm known for my innate ability to play nice

so drip the drunken dimes
into my poor palms tonight
I need a new toy for my devil's hands
that keep looking for a fight...

when you tell the story

arguably
the best part will
remain
the part that
stays untold

that being said
the world is growing miles
by the minute
giant buildings of green folded
enough to cover thousands
of pool tables
soft felt

the twin blades of shoulder
backed into windstorm
a shadow flung high on strings
a village at the foot of a bakingsoda
volcano
waiting for a candy colored
eruption under clouds of applause.

a grey sky and a father's eyes
his words sneak through
the garden's I grew in your head
are not there to hurt you...

we circumnavigate fat cat stomachs
and find fevers that only tourists can find
we bring the strange cats home and watch them eat
domesticated birds

instead of tv
underwater sirens
pull men down by their ankles
some songs can do that
heavier than anchorweight
less forgiving

more likely to return
so for the story's sake
let's call this the scene of the crime

and all these blades of grass were careless weapons
dumped haphazardly in a rash pickupstick moment
beauty is often like that, accidental and disconcerting

we dissected silkworms by moonlight in china
and made fireworks from loud noises
tea from a trembling warmth between our two hands
as you reached for me
and i reached for solace

in holy places, giant stones gather
raise themselves up
in a show of good posture
lean in to whisper about temporary things
and the shapes deceit
likes to dress in
i can't call these days shattered glass anymore
because something stronger started
to crack
and crumble
in the anatomy of a funeral parlor
interchangeably

classroom, church, or courtroom

in the physiology of an exorcism

that the short attention span

of the devil

always walks away from

i have come to tell the time

when daylight is saving

her pennies

to melt down into copper

and give august some color

i have come to seek direction

standing on the compass face

unable to close my aweshaped mouth

but i leave here bound and breathless

bandaged on a board

in an underwater siren

that sounds silent

on a city street.

the hurt of hush

the phone doesn't ring, the floor
creaks under my small broken steps

the heater clicks, chugs
rain pelts window pane, leaves shush
down the sidewalk

cat scratches on the front door
kids ring the bell accidentally
playing dodgeball out front

record spins and lisps a smothered silence
over and over
crows chatter on the telephone wires

the phone doesn't ring, the mailbox is empty
tree branches scrape on the old wooden fence
rain slushes through drain pipes, drips
from the edge of the sagging roof

next door the tv blares through thin walls,
the upstairs neighbors stomp and thud
midnight ticks towards one a.m.

the charms on my bracelet are tinkling as
my hand streaks fancy wet letters across
white wrinkled paper

candles dream up new ways to flicker, wax
oozes gently in pastel colors cascading down
onto an old chipped book case

in the corner of this still, cluttered
room as the carpet cushions the things that lay
dropped, waiting

for a thunder clap, some fireworks, or
even the return of a need
to scream.

www.ingramcontent.com/pod-product-compliance
Lightning Source LLC
Chambersburg PA
CBHW081235090426
42738CB00016B/3314